This LinkedIn Workbook and Planner Belongs to:

If found, contact me here:

Phone: ____________________

Email: ____________________

Address ____________________

Dedicated To

YOU and my clients

Published by
GreyChild Communications
Toronto, ON

LinkedIn Workbook and Planner / Dwainia Grey
ISBN-13: 978-0994888860

ISBN-10: 0994888864

Introduction

WHAT IS THIS?

This is the **LinkedIn Workbook and Planner** that will help you succeed with LinkedIn for your Empowerpreneur business. The book is based on the training in Awesome Nation Engagement; it's a companion book as well as a standalone workbook and planner. The Workbook Section of the book helps you create a LinkedIn strategy for the year and clarify your LinkedIn goals and tactics (action steps). The Planner Section of the book helps you plan your monthly LinkedIn strategy and track your monthly actions and milestones to get a clear picture of your LinkedIn Return on Investment (ROI).

By having a plan you leverage your time, reach targets (people and goals), add automation and measure success.

HOW TO USE THIS WORKBOOK

The first part is the Strategy Workbook which includes worksheets and checklists for you to complete. This helps you develop the LinkedIn Marketing Plan and success strategy for the coming months.

1. Objective
2. Audience
3. Style Guide
4. Engagement in 15 Minutes
5. Do's and Don'ts
6. Planning
7. LinkedIn Post Ideas
8. 52 Weeks
9. LinkedIn Profile Worksheet
10. LinkedIn Page Worksheet
11. LinkedIn Group Worksheet
12. LinkedIn Connections
13. Getting Started Cheat Sheet
14. Blog Stats
15. LinkedIn Yearly Stats

The second section is the **LinkedIn Action Planner**:

1. Monthly Calendar
2. Monthly Success Tracker
3. Monthly Stats
4. Status Updates
5. LinkedIn Campaign Manager
6. To Do
7. Notes

The planner section helps you plan your LinkedIn posts and engagement for the next 12 months. Each month includes monthly planning tools as well as metrics trackers. At the end of each month review the month and start planning for the new month. It's very important to complete your success tracker as it helps you to duplicate success.

The downloadable PDF contains 39 pages and allows you to print pages as needed.

LINKEDIN TODAY

What is the biggest challenge that you are facing right now with LinkedIn?

What do you hope to accomplish?

What have you done so far to get your LinkedIn campaign started?

How much time do you currently spend on LinkedIn a week?

Are you directing LinkedIn fans to your email list?

Are you currently using any of the following tools?

- ☐ LinkedIn
- ☐ Facebook
- ☐ Twitter
- ☐ YouTube
- ☐ Pinterest
- ☐ Google+
- ☐ Instagram
- ☐ Other sites

LinkedIn MARKETING

WORKBOOK

Objective Overall LinkedIn objective for the year.

- Increase reach
- Build your brand
- Engage influencers and connectors
- Increase customer loyalty
- Drive people to events
- Improve customer service
- Generate leads and sales
- Convert leads to sales

Short-term

Goal # 1 –

Deadline

Action Plan

Goal Met ☐ Yes ☐NO

Goal # 2 –

Deadline

Action Plan

Goal Met ☐ Yes ☐NO

Goal # 3 –

Deadline

Action Plan

Goal Met ☐ Yes ☐NO

Long-term

Goal –

Deadline

Action Plan

Goal Met ☐ Yes ☐NO

Monthly Goal Setter

Set realistic achievable goals for each month.
Goals can be a number of posts or number of new followers to engagement. Make sure it's measurable.

January	February
Goal Met ☐ Yes ☐NO	Goal Met ☐ Yes ☐NO
March	April
Goal Met ☐ Yes ☐NO	Goal Met ☐ Yes ☐NO
May	June
Goal Met ☐ Yes ☐NO	Goal Met ☐ Yes ☐NO
July	August
Goal Met ☐ Yes ☐NO	Goal Met ☐ Yes ☐NO
September	October
Goal Met ☐ Yes ☐NO	Goal Met ☐ Yes ☐NO
November	December
Goal Met ☐ Yes ☐NO	Goal Met ☐ Yes ☐NO

Your Audience

- ☐ Existing clients
- ☐ Prospective clients

Where they are hanging out:

- ☐ LinkedIn
- ☐ Twitter
- ☐ Pinterest
- ☐ Instagram
- ☐ Google+
- ☐ Facebook
- ☐
- ☐

Who Are Your Competitors? – How Do They Use LinkedIn? – How Are You Different?

What Keeps Your Client up at Night?

How Does Your Product / Service Solve the Problem?

List 3 Successes You Have Had with Clients
Think RESULTS

What Words or Phrases Do Your Clients Use to Describe The Problem?	What Words or Phrases Do Your Clients Use When They Are Looking for the Solution? (KEYWORD)

Your Avatar

Name (fictitious)

Gender:

Age:

Profession:

Marital and Family Status:

Associations:

Location (city, neighborhood, or zip):

Style Guide

LinkedIn MARKETING

Image Text 1

Font
Size
Style
Color
Hex
RGB
CMYK

Image Text 2

Font
Size
Style
Color
Hex
RGB
CMYK

Watermark Text 1

Font
Size
Style
Color
Hex
RGB
CMYK

Image Sizes

Profile 400 x 400 px
Company Logo 100 x 60
Company Banner 646 x 220
Showcase Page Hero 974 x 330
Showcase Page Logo 400 x 400
Group Logo 100 x 60

Cover Image Template 1400 x 425 px

(paid LinkedIn Account Only)

Post Template 800 x 400 px

Show placement of graphics, watermark, text alignment, borders etc.

Notes

Separate post templates for blog posts, quotes, promotions, etc?

Create templates using Photoshop, Fireworks, Canva or Picmonkey.

Voice, tone, hashtags, abbreviations, spellings and punctuation to use:

15 Minutes A Day of Engagement

	Day 1	Day 2
3-5 Minutes	**Share, like, and comment on other people's content and LinkedIn blog posts.**	**Share, like, and comment on other people's content.**
1-5 Minutes	**Notifications** ☐ Answer Comments (Good and Bad) ☐ Respond to Messages	**Notifications** ☐ Answer Comments (Good and Bad) ☐ Respond to Messages
1-5 Minutes	**Group Interaction** Participate in groups by posting content, answering questions and starting the conversation **Recommend or Endorse** Take time to recommend or endorse a connection on a regular basis.	**Make A New Friend** ☐ Influencers ☐ Current, Past and Future Clients ☐ Future Collaborators ☐ Approve Connection Request

SCHEDULE DAILY STATUS UPDATES

Schedule

- ☐ Schedule other peoples' posts using scheduling tools
- ☐ Schedule your blog posts
- ☐ Day published
- ☐ 1 week later
- ☐ 1 month later

LinkedIn Do's and Don'ts

- ☐ Always follow the rules and regulations for LinkedIn.
- ☐ Do answer all messages / comments in a timely manner.
- ☐ Do commit the time and effort to maintain your LinkedIn marketing plan.
- ☐ Do create a social media marketing plan, but adjust your specific tactics as you go. Be flexible and take the time to find out what works and what doesn't work.
- ☐ Do go local with LinkedIn, it's a great opportunity to take online relationships offline.
- ☐ Do listen to your clients through your social media and respond where appropriate
- ☐ Do participate – join the conversation in groups and by commenting.
- ☐ Do pay attention to social media ethics
- ☐ Do pay attention to the metrics and analytics of your campaign.
- ☐ Do prepare to deal with how online users change, alter or use your brand's message. Have a plan for both good and bad customer feedback.
- ☐ Do support the promotional campaigns of other non-competitive businesses and your connections.
- ☐ Do tag people and companies where appropriate.
- ☐ Remember short posts are better. Add a short description to links. Include images and video.
- ☐ Don't forget to add attribution when it's not your content.
- ☐ Don't just post your own content
- ☐ Don't be disrespectful, offensive, vulgar or use language considered to be inflammatory. Don't be rude or difficult to deal with when engaging with your connections.
- ☐ Don't delete comments unless it's spam. Learn how to deal with negative feedback.
- ☐ Don't lie to your audience or hide the fact that you are advertising to them. Always be transparent with your intentions
- ☐ Don't over post on LinkedIn. Posting 1-2 times a day is good depending on your audience. If you are posting more than 2 times a day ensure it adds value.
- ☐ Don't overdo it when promoting your business. You want to use social media to build relationships not overwhelm people with ads.
- ☐ Don't spam!

Notes

Day-to-Day Management

How many times a week will you post on LinkedIn?
Suggested number of times a week to post: 1x daily

What days and times will you post?

How far ahead do you want to plan content?

How often will you promote your own content (blog posts, events, and products and services) versus other peoples content?

What type of content are you going to share? Review the Post Idea Sheet. What you share needs to bring value - always think "What's in it for me" Try for a combination of education, and engaging. You are aiming to get them interested in you, your brand, and your business.

Who will create content? Images / Video / Copy

Who will post content?

Who will manage your LinkedIn campaigns?

Who will track, monitor and report?

Resources

- ☐ Experienced Writer
- ☐ Professional Photos / Photo shoot
- ☐ Professional Videos / Video shoot
- ☐ Branded Graphics

LinkedIn Policy

Develop your LinkedIn Policy.
Read the Do's and Dont's of LinkedIn. What are the policies you will have for you Empowerpreneur business?

- Rules of engagement
- How to handle customer service
- What to say and what not to say
- Workflow / Schedule
- How to handle negative feedback /criticism
    - Clients, media or competitors

Budget

Startup and launch budget
Campaign budgets
Ongoing management budget

Advertising
Design
Tools (Canva, Pic Monkey, Hootsuite, Buffer, etc)

Metrics

Review your online metrics on a weekly and/or monthly basis. Use Google Analytics in conjunction with bitly, and the LinkedIn Analytics to track and monitor your success. Also use Buffer and Hootsuite reporting tools.

Learn more about your return on investment (ROI – time and money) as well as which posts brings the most traffic, engagement and conversion.

Take time to complete the Blog Stats, Monthly Success Tracker And The Monthly And Yearly Social Media Tracker.
Download the weekly success tracker.

Va Va VooM

Va Va VooM ™ (Content Marketing Ratio)

Value – 60% - Tips, tutorials, and instructional useful and helpful posts

List 3 topics that you can post about that will add value

Visual – 20% - Make use of images and videos

List 3 ways you can use images / videos in social media

Voice – 10% - Show your personality – personal posts about you, showing your life, and a behind the scenes

List 3 posts that will show your personality

Marketing – 10% - Promotional posts to sell and promote your products and services

List 3 products / services you want to sell / promote via social media

Content Ideas for LinkedIn

1	**Valuable & Useful Information**	2	**Blog Posts** Ensure every blog has a branded image	3	**Influencers Posts**	4	**Business News** Updates about your business and industry updates.
5	**Opinions Matter** Ask your LinkedIn Connections opinions on products, services, packaging, new product ideas, promotions, processes etc.	6	**Observations** Relevant to your clients, products / services, blog posts	7	**Tips and Tricks** Post a weekly tip or list.	8	**Events, Workshops and Seminars** Share online and offline events you are hosting or attending
9	**Publications** List and link to any books, articles, or other publication in the designated section	10	**Projects** Post projects you have completed or working on in the designated section	11	**Portfolio** Add images, blog post links, and videos in the designated section	12	**Slideshare** Post presentations and video
13	**Quotes** Post quotes that will motivate and inspire your audience.	14	**Products / Services** Use showcase pages to promote products and services.	15	**Video / Photos** Pictures of you and your products and don't forget people love to watch videos	16	**Questions / Poll** Ask the community what they think
17	**Promotions** Promote your products, services, sales and coupons. Use contests, giveaways and sweepstakes	18	**Honors and Awards** Post updates about honors and awards you and your business have received	19	**Sales** Use LinkedIn Ads for the hard sell; use free resources and tools for the soft sell.	20	**Top Lists** These lists garner more engagement on LinkedIn

Plan out 52 weeks of Tips, Quotes, etc   52 Weeks of ____________________

1		27	
2		28	
3		29	
4		30	
5		31	
6		32	
7		33	
8		34	
9		35	
10		36	
11		37	
12		38	
13		39	
14		40	
15		41	
16		42	
17		43	
18		44	
19		45	
20		46	
21		47	
22		48	
23		49	
24		50	
25		51	
26		52	

LinkedIn Connections

ACCEPT

- ✓ The connection is known and you have a good relationship with them.
- ✓ The connection is not known, but you still have something in common with them such as worked at the same company, from your city, graduated from same school, work in the same industry etc.
- ✓ The connection is not known, but you service the same clients.
- ✓ The connection is not known, but you may be able to offer them help.
- ✓ The connection is not known, but the contact made a personalized invitation, which shows they are interested in getting to know you.

REJECT

- ✗ The connection is known, but you have had bad experiences with them in the past.
- ✗ The connection has an uncompleted profile, no photo and no work experience listed in their profile.
- ✗ The connection is not known and there is nothing in common with either you or your niche.

Search Engine Optimized LinkedIn Profile

Name:

Current and Past Work

Be sure to link your current work with your company page.

Use keywords to get you found.

Education

List your education

Headline

Summary

About You

Other Names:

Favorite Quotes:

Life Events

Work and Education

Family and Relationships

Home and Living

Health and Wellness

Travel and Experience

LinkedIn Page

Objective

Name
Company Name (100 characters)

Purpose of Page
"What's In It for Me?"

Products and Services to Promote

Description (2,000 characters)

LinkedIn Page

Logo 400 x 400 px Logo or Professional Image	Cover Image 646 x 220 px

Settings

- [ ] Company Name
- [ ] Company Description
- [ ] Admins and Direct Sponsored Content Posters
- [ ] Company Type
- [ ] Company Size
- [ ] Company Website
- [ ] Main Company Industry
- [ ] Company Operating Status
- [ ] Year Founded
- [ ] Location up to 5

Optimize Company Page

- [ ] Ensure your Company Page is 100% complete
- [ ] Search Engine Optimized (SEO) your description with keywords
- [ ] Link to Company Page from profile
- [ ] Encourage employees to link to Company Page from their profile
- [ ] Add a Follow Company and/or Company Profile app to your website
- [ ] Promote your LinkedIn Company Page on other social media
- [ ] Share your Company Page with your connections
- [ ] Send a Follow Me on LinkedIn email to your email list
- [ ] Add a link to your Company Page in your email signature

Showcase Page

Consider adding Showcase Pages (up to 10) to showcase different products / services, brand, niche, customers (case studies, testimonials etc) or other. Showcase Pages are mini pages that link back to the main page. They are not linked to a profile page and does not have job / career sections/links. You can build a community around a Showcase Page. Showcase Pages are searchable and has it's own analytics.

Showcase Page Settings

- [ ] Name (100 Characters)
- [ ] Description (200 Characters)
- [ ] Hero Image 974 x 330 px
- [ ] Logo 400 x 400 px

List 10 Showcase Page Ideas

LinkedIn Group

Objective	Name Your Business Name, Service or Product Name, Catchy Name or Name of Your Awesome Nation

Purpose of Group "What's in It for Me?"	Products and Services to Promote

Summary – Brief Description (300 characters)

LinkedIn Group

Description (2,000 characters)

Visibility

☐ Standard – Listed in LinkedIn Group directory and member profile. Members can invite and approve others.

☐ Unlisted – Invisible in members profile and not searchable. Only owners and managers can invite and approve members.

Setup

1. Logo
2. Group Name
3. Summary Description (300 characters)
4. Description (2,000 characters)
5. Website
6. Owner email
7. Visibility
8. Language
9. Location (geographical based group)
10. Group Rules
11. Templates
    - Request to Join Message
    - Welcome Message
    - Decline Message
    - Decline and Block Message

Manage the Group

☐ Welcome new members using the built-in welcome message.

☐ Be natural – You may not agree with all posts , but every post is not for you. People join groups looking for support and affinity. Allow the group to progress, expand and evolve without interference.

☐ Set clear guidelines and rules

☐ Moderate group

☐ Start the conversation: Make Observations, Use Commentary, Ask for Opinions

- ☐ Start a weekly discussion
- ☐ Ask a weekly question

☐ Send a weekly announcement

☐ Appoint other moderators if applicable

LinkedIn Group

Rules

Use your rules section to post guidelines and rules for the group.

- ☐ Discussion topics allowed and not allowed
- ☐ Stance on promotions
- ☐ Stance on spam – what is considered spam?

Group Rules

Moderate Group

- ☐ Review "Moderation Queue"
- ☐ Review "Request to Join"
- ☐ Know what you will and will not allow.
- ☐ Allow members to post.
- ☐ Watch for trolls, spammers and losers.
- ☐ Stick to your rules in the rules section
- ☐ Don't be afraid to remove posts
- ☐ Don't be afraid to remove and block people
- ☐ Be prepared to update rules
- ☐ Create hard and fast rules: Promotion, Hurtful, Threatening, Slandering

Showcase Yourself and Establish Authority

Include your website URL in the group profile, description and welcome message.

Start the conversation

Send a weekly email message to the group.

Promote Your LinkedIn Group

1. Invite connections
2. Promote group on website, blog and newsletter
3. Ensure group name and descriptions is optimized for keywords
4. Encourage group members to invite people
5. Use LinkedIn Ads to promote group
6. Share on other social media
7. Send an email inviting your list

Notes

Getting Started Cheat Sheet

LinkedIn MARKETING

Branding

- ☐ I have a clear description of who my target audience is.
- ☐ My preferred client is using LinkedIn.
- ☐ I have included a professional photo on my personal profile?
- ☐ My LinkedIn Page name is easy to find, follow, and connect with.
    - ☐ It's my business name, brand name or based on an SEO keyword.
    - ☐ It's the same as my other social media profile names for consistency
- ☐ I have a completed LinkedIn Page with a logo?
- ☐ About section includes keywords and website URL - reflects my voice and brand
- ☐ I have claimed my custom LinkedIn URL
- ☐ I know what personality/ brand message and image I want to communicate.
- ☐ I have included a professional email address - @yourwebsite.com
- ☐ I have included my business location (where applicable - at least put country)
- ☐ I ensure I use the correct NAP (Name, Address and Phone number - where applicable)
- ☐ I link to other social media profiles (where applicable)

Planning

- ☐ I know my LinkedIn objective
- ☐ I have defined my LinkedIn marketing goals and know how I will track them.
- ☐ I've created systems to test and track my social media marketing goals and tactics.
- ☐ I have a *Social Media Marketing Plan* that I use to help guide my online marketing and I've integrated my LinkedIn marketing tactics into my overall social media marketing strategies.
- ☐ I've use relevant dashboards and automation tools such as Hootsuite to optimize my time
- ☐ I've documented the systems and tools I use, so it can be easily delegated.
- ☐ I use insights to create targeted posts and know the best day and time for engagement
- ☐ I use LinkedIn Advertising
- ☐ I have a (monthly/ weekly / daily) posting schedule for LinkedIn
- ☐ I have a (monthly/ weekly/ daily) LinkedIn engagement schedule
    - ☐ Post status updates and in groups
    - ☐ Respond to all messages and comments on your page
- ☐ I have a strategy to capture leads from LinkedIn and to get connections to buy

Getting Started Cheat Sheet

LinkedIn MARKETING

Content

- ☐ I have developed a system to find valuable content to share on LinkedIn
- ☐ I make sure I share a good mix of content (*Va Va VooM* – Value, Voice, Visual and Marketing)
- ☐ I use a Call To Action in posts
- ☐ I'm creating specific promotions and offers for my LinkedIn audience - *EXCLUSIVE*.
- ☐ I periodically change my LinkedIn cover photo to highlight my products / services, product launches and promotions
- ☐ I use an editorial calendar to layout content for my blog, and LinkedIn posts.
- ☐ I schedule blog posts as they are published, a week later, and a month later.
- ☐ I create a schedule to promote old blog posts.
- ☐ I use LinkedIn Insights to find the optimal day and time to post content for maximum engagement
- ☐ I follow the top blogs in my industry to stay on top of trends.
- ☐ I create specific content to share on LinkedIn
- ☐ I always check for grammar and spelling

LinkedIn Tools

- ☐ LinkedIn Insights
- ☐ Woobox
- ☐ Hootsuite
- ☐ Buffer
- ☐ Canva
- ☐ Picmonkey
- ☐ Pixlr

LinkedIn Connections

ACCEPT

- ✓ The connection is known and you have a good relationship with them.
- ✓ The connection is not known, but you still have something in common with them such as worked at the same company, from your city, graduated from same school, work in the same industry etc.
- ✓ The connection is not known, but you service the same clients.
- ✓ The connection is not known, but you may be able to offer them help.
- ✓ The connection is not known, but the contact made a personalized invitation, which shows they are interested in getting to know you.

REJECT

- ✗ The connection is known, but you have had bad experiences with them in the past.
- ✗ The connection has an uncompleted profile, no photo and no work experience listed in their profile.
- ✗ The connection is not known and there is nothing in common with either you or your niche.

Blog Stats

	Date	Facebook	Twitter	Google+	Pinterest	Instagram	Blog Visits
1							
2							
3							
4							
5							
6							
7							
8							
9							
10							
11							
12							
13							
14							
15							
16							
17							
18							
19							
20							
21							
22							
23							
24							
25							
26							
27							
28							
29							
30							
31							
32							
33							
34							
35							
36							
37							
38							
39							
40							
41							
42							
43							
44							
45							
46							
47							
48							
49							
50							
51							
52							

Yearly Stats

Year	Total Connections		# of Shares		# of Posts		# of Likes		# of Comments		# of Clicks to Website	
	Goal	Actual	Goal	Actual	Goal	Actual	Goal	Actual	Goal	Actual	Goal	Actual
January												
February												
March												
April												
May												
June												
July												
August												
September												
October												
November												
December												
Yearly Total												

LinkedIn MARKETING

PLANNER

Month

SUNDAY	MONDAY	TUESDAY	WEDNESDAY	THURSDAY	FRIDAY	SATURDAY

Notes

Acknowledge and Celebrate Your Success

Month:

Total Likes

Post with most engagement (shares, likes, comments) on LinkedIn

---

Post with most clicks

Blog post with most traffic from LinkedIn

This month I learned

A record I broke this month

My celebration this month

Next month I plan to do the same

Next month I plan to try (new)

Monthly Stats

GOAL:

Total Connections	New Connections	# of Posts	# of Shares	# of Likes	# of Comments	Reach	# of Clicks	# of Clicks to Website

EMAIL SUBSCRIBERS FROM LINKEDIN	

ENGAGEMENT

Post with most shares	
Post with most likes	
Post with most comments	
Post with most clicks	

SPONSORED POSTS

Spend $	# of Shares	# of Likes	# of Comments	Reach	# of Clicks

LINKEDIN ADS

Spend $		Results	

Status Updates

LinkedIn Status Updates	Date	Time	✓

Campaign Manager

LinkedIn MARKETING

Product / Service Campaign

Campaign	
Description	
Product / Service Newsletter Contest / Giveaway	
Start	End
Objective	
Target Audience	
Budget$ / Cost$ / Return$	
Landing Page	
Tracking Link	
Days and Time	
Winner / Date Notified	

Image

- ☐ Blog Post Announcement
- ☐ Blog Post Follow-up
- ☐ Autoresponder Setup
- ☐ Ad Campaign
  - ○ Budget$
  - ○ Cost$
  - ○ Return$
  - ○ Click Thru Rate
  - ○ CPC (Cost per Click)
- ☐ Conversion Rate
- ☐ Hashtag
- ☐ Coupon Code (if applicable)

Advertising Campaign

Campaign	
Boost / Ad	
Description	
Start	End
Objective	
Target Audience	
Budget$ / Cost Per Day$	
Landing Page	
Tracking Link	

Text	Demographic
	Image

To Do

	Priority	Completed

Month

SUNDAY	MONDAY	TUESDAY	WEDNESDAY	THURSDAY	FRIDAY	SATURDAY

Notes

Acknowledge and Celebrate Your Success

Month:

Total Likes

Post with most engagement (shares, likes, comments) on LinkedIn

---

Post with most clicks

Blog post with most traffic from LinkedIn

This month I learned

A record I broke this month

My celebration this month

Next month I plan to do the same

Next month I plan to try (new)

GOAL:

Total Connections	New Connections	# of Posts	# of Shares	# of Likes	# of Comments	Reach	# of Clicks	# of Clicks to Website

EMAIL SUBSCRIBERS FROM LINKEDIN	
ENGAGEMENT	
Post with most shares	
Post with most likes	
Post with most comments	
Post with most clicks	

SPONSORED POSTS

Spend $	# of Shares	# of Likes	# of Comments	Reach	# of Clicks

LINKEDIN ADS

Spend $		Results	

Status Updates

LinkedIn Status Updates	Date	Time	✓

Campaign Manager

LinkedIn MARKETING

Product / Service Campaign

Campaign	
Description	
Product / Service Newsletter Contest / Giveaway	
Start	End
Objective	
Target Audience	
Budget$ / Cost$ / Return$	
Landing Page	
Tracking Link	
Days and Time	
Winner / Date Notified	

Image

- ☐ Blog Post Announcement
- ☐ Blog Post Follow-up
- ☐ Autoresponder Setup
- ☐ Ad Campaign
  - Budget$
  - Cost$
  - Return$
  - Click Thru Rate
  - CPC (Cost per Click)
- ☐ Conversion Rate
- ☐ Hashtag
- ☐ Coupon Code (if applicable)

Advertising Campaign

Campaign	
Boost / Ad	
Description	
Start	End
Objective	
Target Audience	
Budget$ / Cost Per Day$	
Landing Page	
Tracking Link	

Text	Demographic
	Image

	Priority	Completed

Notes

Calendar

Month

SUNDAY	MONDAY	TUESDAY	WEDNESDAY	THURSDAY	FRIDAY	SATURDAY

Notes

Acknowledge and Celebrate Your Success

Month:

Total Likes

Post with most engagement (shares, likes, comments) on LinkedIn

---

Post with most clicks

Blog post with most traffic from LinkedIn

This month I learned

A record I broke this month

My celebration this month

Next month I plan to do the same

Next month I plan to try (new)

Monthly Stats

GOAL:

Total Connections	New Connections	# of Posts	# of Shares	# of Likes	# of Comments	Reach	# of Clicks	# of Clicks to Website

EMAIL SUBSCRIBERS FROM LINKEDIN	
ENGAGEMENT	
Post with most shares	
Post with most likes	
Post with most comments	
Post with most clicks	

SPONSORED POSTS

Spend $	# of Shares	# of Likes	# of Comments	Reach	# of Clicks

LINKEDIN ADS

Spend $		Results	

LinkedIn Status Updates	Date	Time	✓

Product / Service Campaign

Campaign		
Description		
Product / Service Newsletter Contest / Giveaway		
Start	End	
Objective		
Target Audience		
Budget$ / Cost$ / Return$		
Landing Page		
Tracking Link		
Days and Time		
Winner / Date Notified		

Image

- ☐ Blog Post Announcement
- ☐ Blog Post Follow-up
- ☐ Autoresponder Setup
- ☐ Ad Campaign
  - Budget$
  - Cost$
  - Return$
  - Click Thru Rate
  - CPC (Cost per Click)
- ☐ Conversion Rate
- ☐ Hashtag
- ☐ Coupon Code (if applicable)

Advertising Campaign

Campaign	
Boost / Ad	
Description	
Start	End
Objective	
Target Audience	
Budget$ / Cost Per Day$	
Landing Page	
Tracking Link	

Text	Demographic
	Image

	Priority	Completed

Month

SUNDAY	MONDAY	TUESDAY	WEDNESDAY	THURSDAY	FRIDAY	SATURDAY

Notes

Acknowledge and Celebrate Your Success

Month:

Total Likes

Post with most engagement (shares, likes, comments) on LinkedIn

---

Post with most clicks

Blog post with most traffic from LinkedIn

This month I learned

A record I broke this month

My celebration this month

Next month I plan to do the same

Next month I plan to try (new)

Monthly Stats

GOAL:

Total Connections	New Connections	# of Posts	# of Shares	# of Likes	# of Comments	Reach	# of Clicks	# of Clicks to Website

EMAIL SUBSCRIBERS FROM LINKEDIN	

ENGAGEMENT	
Post with most shares	
Post with most likes	
Post with most comments	
Post with most clicks	

SPONSORED POSTS

Spend $	# of Shares	# of Likes	# of Comments	Reach	# of Clicks

LINKEDIN ADS

Spend $		Results	

Status Updates

LinkedIn Status Updates	Date	Time	✓

Campaign Manager

LinkedIn MARKETING

Product / Service Campaign

Campaign	
Description	
Product / Service Newsletter Contest / Giveaway	
Start	End
Objective	
Target Audience	
Budget$ / Cost$ / Return$	
Landing Page	
Tracking Link	
Days and Time	
Winner / Date Notified	

Image

- ☐ Blog Post Announcement
- ☐ Blog Post Follow-up
- ☐ Autoresponder Setup
- ☐ Ad Campaign
  - Budget$
  - Cost$
  - Return$
  - Click Thru Rate
  - CPC (Cost per Click)
- ☐ Conversion Rate
- ☐ Hashtag
- ☐ Coupon Code (if applicable)

Advertising Campaign

Campaign	
Boost / Ad	
Description	
Start	End
Objective	
Target Audience	
Budget$ / Cost Per Day$	
Landing Page	
Tracking Link	

Text	Demographic

	Image

To Do

	Priority	Completed

Month

SUNDAY	MONDAY	TUESDAY	WEDNESDAY	THURSDAY	FRIDAY	SATURDAY

Notes

Acknowledge and Celebrate Your Success

Month:

Total Likes

Post with most engagement (shares, likes, comments) on LinkedIn

---

Post with most clicks

Blog post with most traffic from LinkedIn

This month I learned

A record I broke this month

My celebration this month

Next month I plan to do the same

Next month I plan to try (new)

Monthly Stats

GOAL:

Total Connections	New Connections	# of Posts	# of Shares	# of Likes	# of Comments	Reach	# of Clicks	# of Clicks to Website

EMAIL SUBSCRIBERS FROM LINKEDIN	

ENGAGEMENT

Post with most shares	
Post with most likes	
Post with most comments	
Post with most clicks	

SPONSORED POSTS

Spend $	# of Shares	# of Likes	# of Comments	Reach	# of Clicks

LINKEDIN ADS

Spend $		Results	

LinkedIn Status Updates	Date	Time	✓

Product / Service Campaign

Campaign	
Description	
Product / Service Newsletter Contest / Giveaway	
Start	End
Objective	
Target Audience	
Budget$ / Cost$ / Return$	
Landing Page	
Tracking Link	
Days and Time	
Winner / Date Notified	

Image

- ☐ Blog Post Announcement
- ☐ Blog Post Follow-up
- ☐ Autoresponder Setup
- ☐ Ad Campaign
  - Budget$
  - Cost$
  - Return$
  - Click Thru Rate
  - CPC (Cost per Click)
- ☐ Conversion Rate
- ☐ Hashtag
- ☐ Coupon Code (if applicable)

Advertising Campaign

Campaign	
Boost / Ad	
Description	
Start	End
Objective	
Target Audience	
Budget$ / Cost Per Day$	
Landing Page	
Tracking Link	

Text	Demographic
	Image

To Do

	Priority	Completed

Month

SUNDAY	MONDAY	TUESDAY	WEDNESDAY	THURSDAY	FRIDAY	SATURDAY

Notes

Acknowledge and Celebrate Your Success

Month:

Total Likes

Post with most engagement (shares, likes, comments) on LinkedIn

---

Post with most clicks

Blog post with most traffic from LinkedIn

This month I learned

A record I broke this month

My celebration this month

Next month I plan to do the same

Next month I plan to try (new)

Monthly Stats

GOAL:

Total Connections	New Connections	# of Posts	# of Shares	# of Likes	# of Comments	Reach	# of Clicks	# of Clicks to Website

EMAIL SUBSCRIBERS FROM LINKEDIN	

ENGAGEMENT	
Post with most shares	
Post with most likes	
Post with most comments	
Post with most clicks	

SPONSORED POSTS

Spend $	# of Shares	# of Likes	# of Comments	Reach	# of Clicks

LINKEDIN ADS

Spend $		Results	

Status Updates

LinkedIn Status Updates	Date	Time	✓

Campaign Manager

LinkedIn MARKETING

Product / Service Campaign

Campaign	
Description	
Product / Service Newsletter Contest / Giveaway	
Start	End
Objective	
Target Audience	
Budget$ / Cost$ / Return$	
Landing Page	
Tracking Link	
Days and Time	
Winner / Date Notified	

Image

- ☐ Blog Post Announcement
- ☐ Blog Post Follow-up
- ☐ Autoresponder Setup
- ☐ Ad Campaign
  - Budget$
  - Cost$
  - Return$
  - Click Thru Rate
  - CPC (Cost per Click)
- ☐ Conversion Rate
- ☐ Hashtag
- ☐ Coupon Code (if applicable)

Advertising Campaign

Campaign	
Boost / Ad	
Description	
Start	End
Objective	
Target Audience	
Budget$ / Cost Per Day$	
Landing Page	
Tracking Link	

Text	Demographic

Image

To Do

	Priority	Completed

Month

SUNDAY	MONDAY	TUESDAY	WEDNESDAY	THURSDAY	FRIDAY	SATURDAY

Notes

Acknowledge and Celebrate Your Success

Month:

Total Likes

Post with most engagement (shares, likes, comments) on LinkedIn

---

Post with most clicks

Blog post with most traffic from LinkedIn

This month I learned

A record I broke this month

My celebration this month

Next month I plan to do the same

Next month I plan to try (new)

Monthly Stats

GOAL:

Total Connections	New Connections	# of Posts	# of Shares	# of Likes	# of Comments	Reach	# of Clicks	# of Clicks to Website

EMAIL SUBSCRIBERS FROM LINKEDIN	
ENGAGEMENT	
Post with most shares	
Post with most likes	
Post with most comments	
Post with most clicks	

SPONSORED POSTS

Spend $	# of Shares	# of Likes	# of Comments	Reach	# of Clicks

LINKEDIN ADS

Spend $		Results	

Status Updates

LinkedIn Status Updates	Date	Time	✓

Campaign Manager

LinkedIn MARKETING

Product / Service Campaign

Campaign	
Description	
Product / Service Newsletter Contest / Giveaway	
Start	End
Objective	
Target Audience	
Budget$ / Cost$ / Return$	
Landing Page	
Tracking Link	
Days and Time	
Winner / Date Notified	

Image

- ☐ Blog Post Announcement
- ☐ Blog Post Follow-up
- ☐ Autoresponder Setup
- ☐ Ad Campaign
  - Budget$
  - Cost$
  - Return$
  - Click Thru Rate
  - CPC (Cost per Click)
- ☐ Conversion Rate
- ☐ Hashtag
- ☐ Coupon Code (if applicable)

Advertising Campaign

Campaign	
Boost / Ad	
Description	
Start	End
Objective	
Target Audience	
Budget$ / Cost Per Day$	
Landing Page	
Tracking Link	

Text	Demographic
	Image

To Do

	Priority	Completed

Month

SUNDAY	MONDAY	TUESDAY	WEDNESDAY	THURSDAY	FRIDAY	SATURDAY

Notes

Acknowledge and Celebrate Your Success

Month:

Total Likes

Post with most engagement (shares, likes, comments) on LinkedIn

---

Post with most clicks

Blog post with most traffic from LinkedIn

This month I learned

A record I broke this month

My celebration this month

Next month I plan to do the same

Next month I plan to try (new)

Monthly Stats

GOAL:

Total Connections	New Connections	# of Posts	# of Shares	# of Likes	# of Comments	Reach	# of Clicks	# of Clicks to Website

EMAIL SUBSCRIBERS FROM LINKEDIN	
ENGAGEMENT	
Post with most shares	
Post with most likes	
Post with most comments	
Post with most clicks	

SPONSORED POSTS

Spend $	# of Shares	# of Likes	# of Comments	Reach	# of Clicks

LINKEDIN ADS

Spend $		Results	

LinkedIn Status Updates	Date	Time	✓

Campaign Manager

LinkedIn MARKETING

Product / Service Campaign

Campaign	
Description	
Product / Service Newsletter Contest / Giveaway	
Start	End
Objective	
Target Audience	
Budget$ / Cost$ / Return$	
Landing Page	
Tracking Link	
Days and Time	
Winner / Date Notified	

Image

- ☐ Blog Post Announcement
- ☐ Blog Post Follow-up
- ☐ Autoresponder Setup
- ☐ Ad Campaign
  - ○ Budget$
  - ○ Cost$
  - ○ Return$
  - ○ Click Thru Rate
  - ○ CPC (Cost per Click)
- ☐ Conversion Rate
- ☐ Hashtag
- ☐ Coupon Code (if applicable)

Advertising Campaign

Campaign	
Boost / Ad	
Description	
Start	End
Objective	
Target Audience	
Budget$ / Cost Per Day$	
Landing Page	
Tracking Link	

Text	Demographic
	Image

To Do

	Priority	Completed

Notes

Month

SUNDAY	MONDAY	TUESDAY	WEDNESDAY	THURSDAY	FRIDAY	SATURDAY

Notes

Acknowledge and Celebrate Your Success

Month:

Total Likes

Post with most engagement (shares, likes, comments) on LinkedIn

---

Post with most clicks

Blog post with most traffic from LinkedIn

This month I learned

A record I broke this month

My celebration this month

Next month I plan to do the same

Next month I plan to try (new)

Monthly Stats

GOAL:

Total Connections	New Connections	# of Posts	# of Shares	# of Likes	# of Comments	Reach	# of Clicks	# of Clicks to Website

EMAIL SUBSCRIBERS FROM LINKEDIN	

ENGAGEMENT

Post with most shares	
Post with most likes	
Post with most comments	
Post with most clicks	

SPONSORED POSTS

Spend $	# of Shares	# of Likes	# of Comments	Reach	# of Clicks

LINKEDIN ADS

Spend $		Results	

Status Updates

LinkedIn Status Updates	Date	Time	✓

Product / Service Campaign

Campaign	
Description	
Product / Service Newsletter Contest / Giveaway	
Start	End
Objective	
Target Audience	
Budget$ / Cost$ / Return$	
Landing Page	
Tracking Link	
Days and Time	
Winner / Date Notified	

Image

- ☐ Blog Post Announcement
- ☐ Blog Post Follow-up
- ☐ Autoresponder Setup
- ☐ Ad Campaign
  - Budget$
  - Cost$
  - Return$
  - Click Thru Rate
  - CPC (Cost per Click)
- ☐ Conversion Rate
- ☐ Hashtag
- ☐ Coupon Code (if applicable)

Advertising Campaign

Campaign	
Boost / Ad	
Description	
Start	End
Objective	
Target Audience	
Budget$ / Cost Per Day$	
Landing Page	
Tracking Link	

Text	Demographic
	Image

To Do

	Priority	Completed

Month

SUNDAY	MONDAY	TUESDAY	WEDNESDAY	THURSDAY	FRIDAY	SATURDAY

Notes

Acknowledge and Celebrate Your Success

Month:

Total Likes

Post with most engagement (shares, likes, comments) on LinkedIn

---

Post with most clicks

Blog post with most traffic from LinkedIn

This month I learned

A record I broke this month

My celebration this month

Next month I plan to do the same

Next month I plan to try (new)

Monthly Stats

GOAL:

Total Connections	New Connections	# of Posts	# of Shares	# of Likes	# of Comments	Reach	# of Clicks	# of Clicks to Website

EMAIL SUBSCRIBERS FROM LINKEDIN	

ENGAGEMENT

Post with most shares	
Post with most likes	
Post with most comments	
Post with most clicks	

SPONSORED POSTS

Spend $	# of Shares	# of Likes	# of Comments	Reach	# of Clicks

LINKEDIN ADS

Spend $		Results	

LinkedIn Status Updates	Date	Time	✓

Product / Service Campaign

Campaign	
Description	
Product / Service Newsletter Contest / Giveaway	
Start	End
Objective	
Target Audience	
Budget$ / Cost$ / Return$	
Landing Page	
Tracking Link	
Days and Time	
Winner / Date Notified	

Image

- ☐ Blog Post Announcement
- ☐ Blog Post Follow-up
- ☐ Autoresponder Setup
- ☐ Ad Campaign
  - Budget$
  - Cost$
  - Return$
  - Click Thru Rate
  - CPC (Cost per Click)
- ☐ Conversion Rate
- ☐ Hashtag
- ☐ Coupon Code (if applicable)

Advertising Campaign

Campaign	
Boost / Ad	
Description	
Start	End
Objective	
Target Audience	
Budget$ / Cost Per Day$	
Landing Page	
Tracking Link	

Text	Demographic
	Image

To Do

	Priority	Completed

Month

SUNDAY	MONDAY	TUESDAY	WEDNESDAY	THURSDAY	FRIDAY	SATURDAY

Notes

Acknowledge and Celebrate Your Success

Month:

Total Likes

Post with most engagement (shares, likes, comments) on LinkedIn

---

Post with most clicks

Blog post with most traffic from LinkedIn

This month I learned

A record I broke this month

My celebration this month

Next month I plan to do the same

Next month I plan to try (new)

Monthly Stats

GOAL:

Total Connections	New Connections	# of Posts	# of Shares	# of Likes	# of Comments	Reach	# of Clicks	# of Clicks to Website

EMAIL SUBSCRIBERS FROM LINKEDIN	
ENGAGEMENT	
Post with most shares	
Post with most likes	
Post with most comments	
Post with most clicks	

SPONSORED POSTS

Spend $	# of Shares	# of Likes	# of Comments	Reach	# of Clicks

LINKEDIN ADS

Spend $		Results	

Status Updates

LinkedIn Status Updates	Date	Time	✓

Campaign Manager

Product / Service Campaign

Campaign	
Description	
Product / Service Newsletter Contest / Giveaway	
Start	End
Objective	
Target Audience	
Budget$ / Cost$ / Return$	
Landing Page	
Tracking Link	
Days and Time	
Winner / Date Notified	

Image

- ☐ Blog Post Announcement
- ☐ Blog Post Follow-up
- ☐ Autoresponder Setup
- ☐ Ad Campaign
  - ○ Budget$
  - ○ Cost$
  - ○ Return$
  - ○ Click Thru Rate
  - ○ CPC (Cost per Click)
- ☐ Conversion Rate
- ☐ Hashtag
- ☐ Coupon Code (if applicable)

Advertising Campaign

Campaign	
Boost / Ad	
Description	
Start	End
Objective	
Target Audience	
Budget$ / Cost Per Day$	
Landing Page	
Tracking Link	

Text

Demographic

Image

To Do

	Priority	Completed

Month

SUNDAY	MONDAY	TUESDAY	WEDNESDAY	THURSDAY	FRIDAY	SATURDAY

Notes

Acknowledge and Celebrate Your Success

Month:

Total Likes

Post with most engagement (shares, likes, comments) on LinkedIn

Post with most clicks

Blog post with most traffic from LinkedIn

This month I learned

A record I broke this month

My celebration this month

Next month I plan to do the same

Next month I plan to try (new)

Monthly Stats

GOAL:

Total Connections	New Connections	# of Posts	# of Shares	# of Likes	# of Comments	Reach	# of Clicks	# of Clicks to Website

EMAIL SUBSCRIBERS FROM LINKEDIN	
ENGAGEMENT	
Post with most shares	
Post with most likes	
Post with most comments	
Post with most clicks	

SPONSORED POSTS

Spend $	# of Shares	# of Likes	# of Comments	Reach	# of Clicks

LINKEDIN ADS

Spend $		Results	

LinkedIn Status Updates	Date	Time	✓

Campaign Manager

LinkedIn MARKETING

Product / Service Campaign

Campaign	
Description	
Product / Service Newsletter Contest / Giveaway	
Start	End
Objective	
Target Audience	
Budget$ / Cost$ / Return$	
Landing Page	
Tracking Link	
Days and Time	
Winner / Date Notified	

Image

- ☐ Blog Post Announcement
- ☐ Blog Post Follow-up
- ☐ Autoresponder Setup
- ☐ Ad Campaign
  - Budget$
  - Cost$
  - Return$
  - Click Thru Rate
  - CPC (Cost per Click)
- ☐ Conversion Rate
- ☐ Hashtag
- ☐ Coupon Code (if applicable)

Advertising Campaign

Campaign	
Boost / Ad	
Description	
Start	End
Objective	
Target Audience	
Budget$ / Cost Per Day$	
Landing Page	
Tracking Link	

Text	Demographic

Image

	Priority	Completed

HOPE YOU ENJOYED USING
YOUR LINKEDIN WORKBOOK AND PLANNER

GET YOUR FREE WEEKLY LINKEDIN PLANNER!
http://bit.ly/linkedinweekly

PLEASE LEAVE A REVIEW ON AMAZON

BE SURE TO GRAB YOUR COPIES
- Social Media Marketing Workbook -
- Social Media Marketing Planner -
- Google+ Workbook and Planner -
- Facebook Workbook and Planner -
- Twitter Workbook and Planner -
- Pinterest Workbook and Planner -
- Instagram Workbook and Planner -

ALSO LOOK OUT FOR
Authentic Marketing – The Three E's of Online Marketing: Ethical, Effortless, Engaging
Social Media Marketing: How to Master Engagement in 15 Minutes a Day.

Connect with Dwainia Grey on LinkedIn, Google+, Facebook, Twitter, Pinterest and Instagram
dwainiagrey.me

Made in the USA
Middletown, DE
05 November 2026

36545328R10077